Celebrating Our Holidays

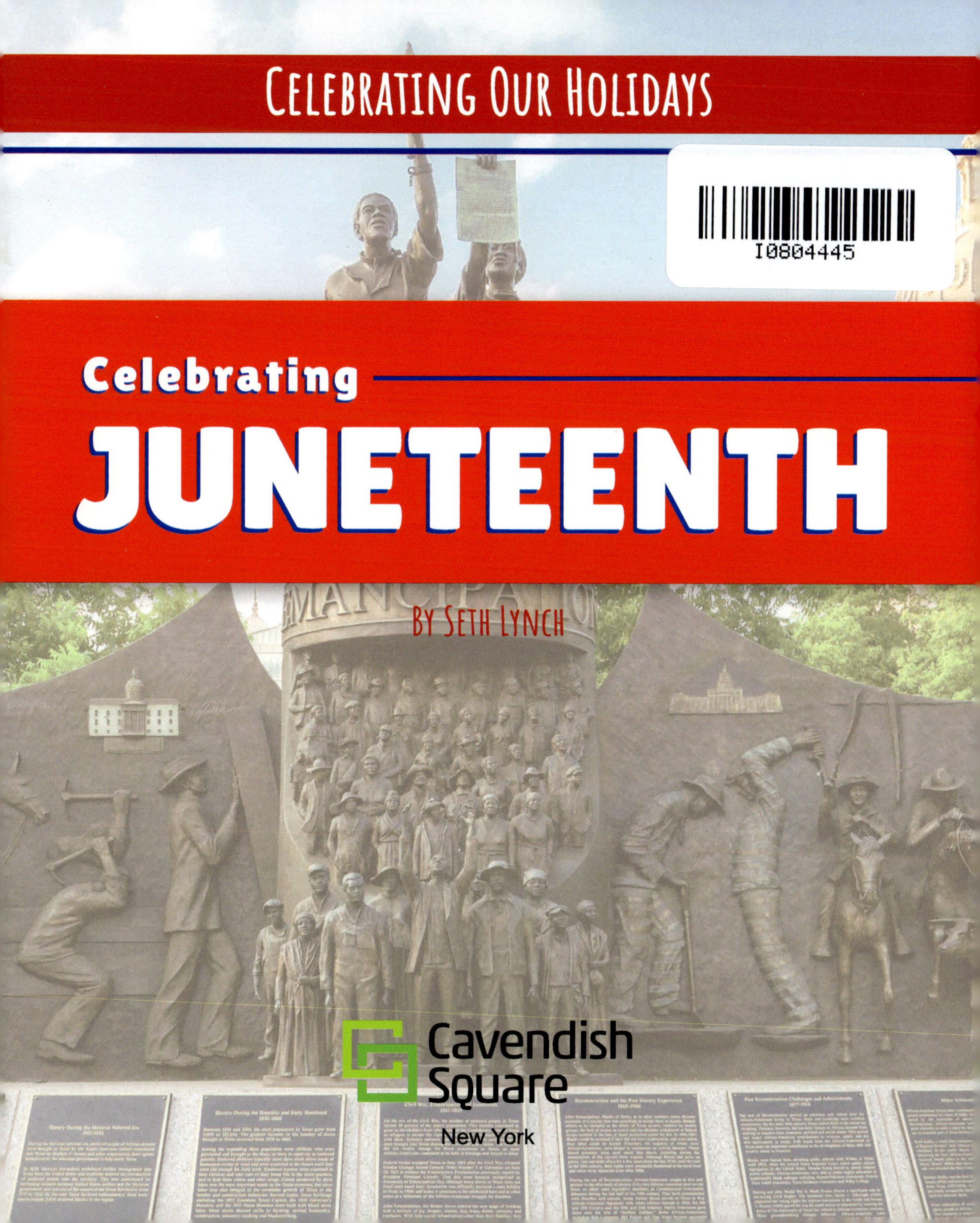

# Celebrating JUNETEENTH

By Seth Lynch



Cavendish Square
New York

Published in 2023 by Cavendish Square Publishing, LLC
29 E. 21st Street New York, NY 10010



First Edition



Library of Congress Cataloging-in-Publication Data

Names: Lynch, Seth, author.
Title: Celebrating Juneteenth / Seth Lynch.
Description: New York : Cavendish Square Publishing, [2023] | Series: Celebrating our holidays | Includes index.
Identifiers: LCCN 2021042185 | ISBN 9781502665058 (set) | ISBN 9781502665065 (library binding) | ISBN 9781502665041 (paperback) | ISBN 9781502665072 (ebook)
Subjects: LCSH: Juneteenth–Juvenile literature. | Slaves–Emancipation–Texas–Juvenile literature. | African Americans–Anniversaries, etc.–Juvenile literature. | African Americans–Social life and customs–Juvenile literature.
Classification: LCC E185.93.T4 L96 2023 | DDC 394.263–dc23
LC record available at https://lccn.loc.gov/2021042185

Editor: Kristen Nelson
Copyeditor: Jill Keppeler
Designer: Deanna Paternostro

The photographs in this book are used by permission and through the courtesy of: Cover pp. 1 Moab Republic/Shutterstock.com; back cover, pp. 3, 5, 7, 9, 13, 15, 16, 19, 20, 23, 27, 28, 29, 30, 31, 32 N.D.Vector/Shutterstock.com; pp. 4, 24 American Photo Archive/Alamy Stock Photo; p. 6 EvgeniiAnd/Shutterstock.com; pp. 8, 11, 16 Everett Collection/Shutterstock.com; p. 10 Rainer Lesniewski/Shutterstock.com; p. 14 Niday Picture Library/Alamy Stock Photo; p. 17 MediaPunch Inc/Alamy Stock Photo; p. 18 Aaron of L.A. Photography/Shutterstock.com; p. 20 Linda Hughes Photography/Shutterstock.com; pp. 21, 22 Tippman98x/Shutterstock.com; p. 26 Fiora Watts/Shutterstock.com; pp. 28 (left), 29 (right) Olga_Shestakova/Shutterstock.com; p. 28 (right) Mega Pixel/Shutterstock.com; p. 29 (left) Radu Bercan/Shutterstock.com



CPSIA compliance information: Batch #CSCSQ23: For further information contact Cavendish Square Publishing LLC, New York, New York, at 1-877-980-4450.

Printed in the United States of America

# CONTENTS

**Vice President Kamala Harris, the first Black American to be vice president, was present as the president made Juneteenth a nationally recognized holiday. She said, "We have come far and we have far to go, but today is a day of celebration."**

# CHAPTER ONE

## A New National Holiday

On June 17, 2021, Juneteenth became just the 12th U.S. federal, or national, holiday. President Joe Biden signed a bill into law that day, officially recognizing the long-celebrated day of **emancipation**. Juneteenth has been celebrated on June 19 since 1865, when people in the last state left to find out were brought word that the American Civil War had ended and that the **enslaved** people there were free. Over time, the date has sometimes been called Freedom Day or Emancipation Day. However, to most Black Americans today, the date is simply called Juneteenth. "Juneteenth" is a combination of the two parts of the date: "June" and "nineteenth."

The idea to make Juneteenth a national holiday has been around since at least the 1950s and 1960s. This was during the U.S. civil rights movement, a time when Black people started an increased push for equal rights. Texas made Juneteenth an official state holiday in 1980. By 2021, most other states had officially recognized the holiday too.

Nonetheless, a large percentage of Americans are still unaware of the history of Juneteenth. Some schools have included it in their classroom learning, and it's a joyful holiday in Black **culture**. However, to some, President Biden's

**Many holidays are tied to a particular faith. Juneteenth is a nonreligious holiday that has become an important day in Black culture—and American culture in general.**

## Coming Together

In June 2020, interest in Juneteenth hit a modern peak, shown by the spike in Google searches and Twitter mentions of Juneteenth that month. This likely occurred because of widespread protests against the way police treat people of color, particularly Black people. Juneteenth became a day on which Black Americans could come together in whatever ways they were able, despite the fight against **discrimination** that continues around the country.

introduction of a new national holiday was the first they'd ever heard of Juneteenth. Black Americans and their history have long been ignored in many cases, and the history of this holiday and what it stands for are important for all Americans to understand.

At its center, Juneteenth is a celebration of freedom. It's a holiday that can help connect Black Americans today with the history of enslaved people in the United States. It encourages people to come together and work toward a future where freedom means more than just not being enslaved. It means equality.

The first enslaved people were brought to the present-day United States from Africa during the 1500s and 1600s.

# CHAPTER TWO

## War Leads to Freedom

The origins of Juneteenth date back more than 150 years. The holiday began following a war within the United States. One of the outcomes of the war was freedom for enslaved people. In some places, like Texas, that freedom was held up by both the slow means of communication of the time and by those who didn't want to free their enslaved workers.

### Slavery Leads to War

From 1861 to 1865, the United States fought the Civil War, largely over the issue of slavery. Conflict about slavery had been raging for years. By this time, for the most part, people in mostly Northern states opposed its spread to the new, western territories being added to the United States. Those in mostly Southern states wanted to continue their use of enslaved people. They said the U.S. government shouldn't be able to decide whether slavery was allowed in a new state. For a time, no new states allowing slavery could be added to the United States north of the southern border of Missouri. Then, in 1854, the Kansas-Nebraska Act allowed the people in two new territories above that line to choose whether they wanted to allow slavery.

**Shown here is a map of the Union and Confederate states in 1863.**

Abraham Lincoln was elected president in 1860. He was part of the Republican Party, which opposed slavery. Many states saw his election as a blow to slavery, which held up some states' economies. These states began to secede from, or leave, the Union. Soon, 11 states had left and joined to create the Confederate States of America: South Carolina, Arkansas, Mississippi, Florida, Alabama, Georgia, Tennessee, North Carolina, Virginia, Louisiana, and Texas.

## The Proclamation

A long, bloody war began when shots were fired on the Union-held Fort Sumter in South Carolina on April 12, 1861. As the fighting continued,

President Lincoln looked for ways to bring the country back together. In September 1862, he issued what's now called the preliminary proclamation. It stated that if the Confederate states didn't rejoin the United States, Lincoln would free all enslaved people in those states on January 1, 1863. The Confederate states refused, so Lincoln signed the Emancipation Proclamation. It freed all the enslaved people in the Confederate states. It also allowed Black men, including enslaved men who had been freed, to join the Union army or navy.

**During the Civil War, about 180,000 Black men fought for the Union. Some were free Black men and others were enslaved men who escaped or were freed as the Union began to win in the South.**

While it was a big step toward the end of slavery, the Emancipation Proclamation only freed the enslaved people in Confederate states. That meant states that hadn't seceded didn't have to free those who were enslaved. The proclamation also didn't apply to parts of the Confederate states that had already been taken by the Union army. In addition, since the Confederate states weren't going to enforce the proclamation, many enslaved people remained enslaved until Union troops freed them by defeating Confederate troops. The only way all enslaved people in the South would be freed would be if the Union won the whole war.

That made the Emancipation Proclamation a declaration of hope. Now, the Union troops were seen as fighting for the freedom of those who were enslaved in the Confederacy—and those who were enslaved finally saw a path to freedom.

## The Slow End of Slavery

The Civil War ended, for the most part, on April 9, 1865. For many enslaved people, slavery had ended with the Emancipation Proclamation more than two years earlier. However, in some places, enslaved people didn't even know about the proclamation. Enslavers in those places may have known about it, but they didn't want to lose—or pay—those who were enslaved. Galveston, Texas, was one of those places.

General Gordon Granger and a large force of Union troops marched into Galveston on June 19, 1865. Granger read a document called General Order Number 3. It stated:

> *The people of Texas are informed that, in accordance with a proclamation from the Executive of the United States, all slaves are free. This involves an absolute equality of personal rights and rights of property between former masters and slaves, and*

## Truly Free?

The Emancipation Proclamation, and then General Order Number 3, freed the enslaved people of Texas. However, that didn't mean that every one of them was truly free even after those official words were shared. Some enslavers still didn't let enslaved people go until someone from the government forced them to. They wanted to wait until the end of the harvest season. Enslaved people who tried to push for their right to freedom were often hurt or killed.

*the connection heretofore existing between them becomes that between employer and hired labor.*

The 250,000 enslaved people in Texas were officially free. Those who could do so celebrated by gathering together. They sang, danced, and had feasts.

## The 13th Amendment

When President Lincoln signed the Emancipation Proclamation, he knew it wouldn't be enough to end slavery in the United States. However, he was **assassinated** on April 14, 1865, before he could see the states ratify, or approve, an **amendment** to the U.S. Constitution to end slavery. Slavery in the United States was abolished, or ended, with the ratification of the 13th Amendment in December 1865. Formerly enslaved people as well as their **descendants** were free under the law. June 19, the day Texas's enslaved people were told of their freedom, became a celebration of that freedom.

Juneteenth celebrations were often difficult to hold in the early years of the holiday. Here, a group gathers for Juneteenth in 1900.

# CHAPTER THREE

## EARLY JUNETEENTH CELEBRATIONS

It's surprising that newly freed Black Americans in Texas were able to celebrate on June 19, 1865, or even the year after. Former captors of enslaved people had been slow to give them the news of their freedom and even made them continue to work in some cases. Furthermore, even though slavery had ended, more equal treatment for Black Americans was a long way off. Nonetheless, against the odds, Juneteenth became an annual celebration. This shows just how much it meant to formerly enslaved people, their descendants, and Black Americans today.

### THE FIRST CELEBRATIONS

Enslaved people who were freed in 1865 in Texas celebrated on June 19 if they could. In 1866, celebrations occurred on that date again. Families got together and prayed. They sang **spirituals**. Juneteenth was celebrated in the coming years in Texas through public readings of the Emancipation Proclamation, church services, and food, including barbecue. People sometimes discussed voting rights. Formerly enslaved people and their families often traveled to Galveston for Juneteenth to revisit the place where freedom was first declared in Texas.

Juneteenth spread beyond Texas as formerly enslaved people and their descendants moved to other states. While not all Black Americans had found out about freedom on June 19, 1865, the date often felt meaningful to them. It became the day on which general emancipation was celebrated.

## JUNETEENTH STALLS

In some states, Black people were kept from gathering in certain public places—or in public at all. When that happened, those who celebrated Juneteenth held their events in homes or near rivers and lakes, away

### THE SUPREME COURT RULES

After the Civil War, Black Americans were full citizens of the United States. However, due to Jim Crow laws, they didn't have all the rights that should have included. In 1954, the Supreme Court ruled segregation in public schools was illegal. Its decision stated that separate buildings and schools for Black people were, in truth, not equal. The court case, *Brown v. Board of Education of Topeka*, was the first major blow to Jim Crow laws.

**Jim Crow laws were in effect across the South from the 1870s until the 1950s.**

from towns. This only got harder as discriminatory laws called Jim Crow laws were passed in many Southern states, including Texas. These laws made it illegal for Black people to share many spaces, including schools, bathrooms, and restaurants, with white people. The official separation of Black people and white people is called segregation.

As white people passed more Jim Crow laws and segregation continued into the 1900s, Juneteenth became harder and harder to celebrate. By the time World War II (1939–1945) broke out, observance of the holiday had significantly decreased. Then, the civil rights movement began to spread as Black Americans pushed for more equality.

In 1968, shortly after the assassination of civil rights leader Martin Luther King Jr., Black leaders held events in Washington, D.C., to make more people aware of economic inequality in the United States. One of these was Solidarity Day, which was held on June 19. Thousands of people were there and took their new knowledge of Juneteenth home. After that, Juneteenth celebrations began to pop up around the United States. It gained so much recognition that calls for it to become a national holiday began soon after.

**Shown here is Coretta Scott King—the wife of Martin Luther King Jr. She helped his message of equality for Black Americans live on after his death.**

**People gather to raise the Juneteenth flag to begin their celebration of the holiday.**

# CHAPTER FOUR

## A SYMBOLIC HOLIDAY

Juneteenth is a symbol itself. It symbolizes, or stands for, the freedom gained by Black Americans through the Emancipation Proclamation and the end of the Civil War. Like many other holidays, people decorate for Juneteenth. The most well-known part of Juneteenth displays is the Juneteenth flag. It represents justice and freedom for all Black Americans.

### A FLAG OF SYMBOLS

The Juneteenth flag was created mainly by an **activist** named Ben Haith in 1997. An illustrator named Lisa Jeanne Graf brought his idea to life. Three years later, it was updated to look as it does today. Then, in 2007, the date of the first Juneteenth was added: June 19, 1865.

Haith chose the colors and other shapes on the flag to show certain meanings. The top of the flag is a brilliant blue. The bottom half is bright red. Like the U.S. flag, the Juneteenth flag also features white. The red, white, and blue are meant to call to mind the U.S. flag and to remind everyone who sees it that formerly enslaved people and their families were and are Americans.

The arc, or curve, where the blue and red meet on the flag has meaning too. It stands for new horizons, or opportunities for Black Americans in the future.

In the center of the flag is a white star. It has two meanings. First, it symbolizes Texas, which is sometimes called the Lone Star State. The official Texas state flag also features a large, white star. The star also stands for freedom for all Black American in all 50 of the states.

Around the star is a white burst. Haith has said a nova, or an event in which in star or stars shine brightly, inspired the burst. The burst symbolizes the new beginnings emancipation brought to the Black people in Galveston and in the rest of the United States.

## Juneteenth Decorations

The more Juneteenth spreads, the more decorations have become available in major stores. Wal-Mart, Amazon.com, and Party City all carry Juneteenth decorations. Handmade and specialty items can be found on

## Juneteenth and Kente Cloth

The red, yellow, green, and black of many Juneteenth decorations are often shown woven together. This represents a special fabric called kente cloth. Real kente cloth is woven by hand in Africa, most often in Ghana. Today, those looking to show their pride in having African roots may wear it—even though most fabric that looks like kente cloth is unlikely to have actually been made in Africa.

**Kente cloth can have any group of colors. First made thousands of years ago, it used to be just for royalty to wear.**

**Many Americans show their participation in the holiday of Juneteenth through what they wear.**

Etsy. Pinterest is full of ideas and projects people can use to make their own themed decorations.

Many decorations feature the Juneteenth flag, but the colors seen most aren't red, white, and blue. They're often red, green, yellow, and black. These colors are often used to represent African **heritage**. Juneteenth decorations often feature phrases supporting Black culture and pride.

It's also possible to find special shirts and hats to wear on Juneteenth. Wearing clothing or putting up decorations can be especially important in the case of Juneteenth because it showcases a lesser-known holiday for those who may not know about it. Additionally, those wearing Juneteenth-themed clothing and putting up decorations can more easily spot others who are also celebrating, bringing a sense of community during Juneteenth.

Juneteenth parades, like this one in Philadelphia, Pennsylvania, are common across the United States.

# CHAPTER FIVE

## JUNETEENTH TODAY

Juneteenth celebrations remain an important part of Black culture today. With its recognition as a national holiday, Juneteenth will only become more a part of American culture in general. As people of all backgrounds learn about this holiday, they can have more conversations about what Black people have gone through in their history—and what they continue to go through today.

### JOYFUL JUNETEENTH

Juneteenth has long been celebrated with family get-togethers, barbecues, and music. Many cities also have a Juneteenth parade or other festivities like concerts and dance shows. The Juneteenth Music Festival in Denver, Colorado, featured music acts, street performers, and a street fair, among other events, in June 2021. A Juneteenth Freedom Days event was celebrated in a state park near Pittsburgh, Pennsylvania, in June 2021 too. Music performances, including a battle of the bands, were the highlight.

**Opal Lee (*seated*) was present when President Biden made Juneteenth a national holiday.**

During Juneteenth celebrations, speakers may talk about the history of Juneteenth or share facts about the importance of voting. In 2021, Opal Lee spoke in Fort Worth, Texas, at the Juneteenth parade. Lee, called the Grandmother of Juneteenth, worked for 40 years to bring attention to the holiday and have it nationally recognized. After walking 2.5 miles (4 kilometers), the 94-year-old Lee spoke with hope about Juneteenth becoming a federal holiday. She said it was the beginning of the people of America working together as one: "It's not a white thing. It's not a Black thing. It's an American thing."

## A Holiday of the Moment

The death of George Floyd in May 2020 sparked protests across the United States. Floyd was a Black man killed by a white police officer in Minneapolis, Minnesota. The deaths of Floyd and others that year highlighted the unequal and often harsh treatment of people of color, particularly Black people, in the justice system.

In the midst of these protests and events, many people found Juneteenth to have an even greater meaning. The holiday was a unifying event for Black Americans, as shown by the increase in social media mentions of the day in 2020. Big companies such as Nike, Target, and the National Football League (NFL) gave their employees a paid holiday for Juneteenth.

All of this made Juneteenth more visible. Many felt this was a good thing, not just for the holiday but for the further education of the people of the United States.

## An Ongoing Conversation

When people talk about Juneteenth on social media or the news, it sparks conversations about what the holiday is. Then, people can discuss its history—and what that history means to the events

**The Black Lives Matter organization was a big part of the protests in 2020. This group fights against violence toward Black people and injustices faced by Black communities.**

## Do We Still Need Juneteenth?

Al Edwards was a Texas politician and activist who headed the bill to make Juneteenth a Texas state holiday. In 2007, he spoke about why Juneteenth should be celebrated, even more than a century after emancipation: "Every year we must remind **successive** generations that this event [caused] a series of events that one by one defines the challenges and responsibilities of successive generations."

of the present. Having conversations with friends and family about the origins, or roots, of Juneteenth can remind them of the struggles Black Americans faced and continue to face. Sometimes conversations about race can feel uncomfortable, but the joyful celebration of freedom that is Juneteenth is a great way to start those talks.

Juneteenth has been celebrated for more than 150 years and is gaining strength today. People of all backgrounds can celebrate this "second independence day" for the United States each June 19, especially now that it's a national holiday. Additionally, all Americans can carry the knowledge of Juneteenth all year and find ways to uplift those who have been mistreated. That may include supporting Black-owned businesses, attending a protest against unjust voting laws, or simply talking about ways to be **antiracist** with family and friends. Juneteenth is a holiday of unity and freedom. You can help make it a holiday of equality!

## Make a Cardboard Juneteenth Flag

### You Will Need:

cardboard box
red and blue paint
glue
foam paintbrush
scissors
pencil
painter's tape
white cardstock

**Show your Juneteenth pride with this flag craft. Shown here are some of the things you'll need.**

## DIRECTIONS:

1. Use scissors to cut a piece of recycled cardboard into a rectangle.
2. Put a piece of painter's tape across the middle of the cardboard. Paint the top half blue. Let the paint dry, and remove the tape.
3. Paint the bottom half of the cardboard red. Let the paint dry.
4. Draw the star and starburst of the Juneteenth flag on your piece of white cardstock, or find a picture of these symbols and print them out on white cardstock. Cut both out using scissors.
5. Glue the star to the middle of the flag. Next, glue the starburst around the star. Hang your Juneteenth flag in the window!

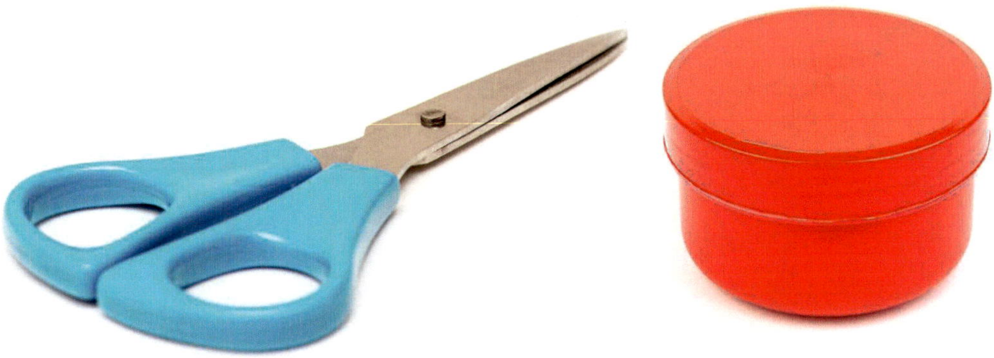

# GLOSSARY

**activist:** One who acts strongly in support of or against an issue or cause.

**amendment:** A change or addition to a constitution.

**antiracist:** Opposed to racism, or the belief that people of different races have different qualities and abilities and that some are superior or inferior.

**assassinate:** To kill someone, especially a public figure.

**culture:** The customs, beliefs, and ways of life of a group of people.

**descendant:** Someone related to someone from an earlier time.

**discrimination:** Unfairly treating people unequally because of their race or beliefs.

**emancipation:** The act of freeing from the restraint, control, or power of another, usually referring to the freeing of enslaved people.

**enslaved:** Having to do with being treated as another person's property and forced to work without pay.

**heritage:** The traditions and beliefs that are part of the history of a group or nation.

**spiritual:** A song of great feeling having to do with faith and most commonly associated with Black culture.

**successive:** Following after another in a series.

# FIND OUT MORE

## Books

Cooper, Floyd. *Juneteenth for Mazie*. North Mankato, MN: Capstone Editions, a Capstone Imprint, 2021.

Shaffer, Jody Jenson. *Celebrating Juneteenth*. Mankato, MN: The Child's World, 2021.

Wyeth, Sharon Dennis. *Juneteenth: Our Day of Freedom*. New York, NY: Random House Children's Books, 2022.

## Websites

**Colonial America for Kids: Slavery**
*www.ducksters.com/history/colonial_america/slavery.php*
Review the facts about slavery in U.S. history here.

**Emancipation Proclamation**
*www.dkfindout.com/us/history/american-civil-war/emancipation-proclamation/*
Discover more about the Emancipation Proclamation and the Civil War with this interactive timeline.

**National Holidays Around the World**
*www.scholastic.com/teachers/articles/teaching-content/national-holidays-around-world/*
Other countries celebrate different holidays from the United States! Read about more of them on Scholastic's website.

**Publisher's note to educators and parents:** Our editors have carefully reviewed these websites to ensure that they are suitable for students. Many websites change frequently, however, and we cannot guarantee that a site's future contents will continue to meet our high standards of quality and educational value. Be advised that students should be closely supervised whenever they access the internet.

# INDEX